The Forest Friends

The Forest Friends

A TALE OF FRIENDSHIP AND UNITY

Anurag Anurag

Aman Nanavaty

Contents

1

The Forest Awakens

The sun slowly climbed over the horizon, spreading its golden rays through the tall trees of the dense forest. The morning light made everything glow, and the forest woke up with a burst of colors and sounds. Birds chirped cheerfully, and the leaves rustled gently in the soft breeze.

In this beautiful forest, many animals lived happily. Among them were four special creatures: Wolf, Deer, Snake, and Eagle. Each had their own story and place in the forest.

Wolf, with his thick fur and sharp teeth, was cunning and always on the lookout for food. He had tried many times to catch Deer, who was swift and graceful, always managing to escape just in time.

"Today will be the day," Wolf muttered to himself as he trotted through the underbrush, his eyes scanning for any sign of Deer.

Meanwhile, Deer was enjoying a peaceful morning near a sparkling river. The grass was fresh and green, and colorful flowers bloomed all around. Deer nibbled on the sweet grass, his large eyes always alert for any movement.

"I must be careful," Deer whispered to himself, his ears twitching. "Wolf might be nearby."

High above, Eagle soared through the sky, his keen eyes watching everything below. He was majestic and powerful, always looking for his next meal. For years, he had been hunting Snake, who was wise and elusive.

"Where could Snake be hiding today?" Eagle wondered as he circled over the treetops.

Down on the forest floor, Snake slithered silently through the grass, his scales shimmering in the sunlight. He knew Eagle was searching for him, so he moved carefully, blending in with his surroundings.

"I must stay hidden," Snake thought, flicking his tongue to taste the air. "Eagle might be hunting me."

The forest was a place of beauty and danger, where each animal had to be clever to survive. But it was also a place where friendships could form, even among those who seemed like enemies.

As the sun climbed higher in the sky, the forest buzzed with life.

Squirrels chattered as they gathered nuts, and rabbits hopped through the underbrush. The air was filled with the sweet scent of flowers and the sound of running water from the river.

Wolf continued his search, his nose twitching as he sniffed the air. "I will find Deer today," he said determinedly.

Deer, sensing Wolf's presence, decided to move to a safer spot. "I must stay ahead of him," Deer thought as he gracefully bounded through the forest, his hooves barely making a sound.

Snake, feeling the warmth of the sun, decided to rest for a while. He coiled up in a sunny spot, keeping a watchful eye on the sky. "I must stay alert," he reminded himself.

Eagle, still soaring high, decided to take a break on a tall tree branch. He spread his wings wide, enjoying the view of the forest below. "I will catch Snake one day," he said confidently.

The forest, with its tall trees and clear river, was a place of adventure and wonder. And as the day went on, the four creatures continued their lives, each facing their own challenges and dreaming their own dreams.

In this lush woodland, the sun's golden glow brought warmth and light, reminding all the creatures that every day was a new chance to live, learn, and maybe even find unexpected friendships.

2

The Wolf's Hunger

The forest was alive with the sounds of chirping birds and rustling leaves. The air was fresh, filled with the scent of pine and wildflowers. As the sun climbed higher in the sky, Wolf prowled through the dense underbrush, his eyes gleaming with determination.

Wolf had always dreamed of catching Deer. Despite countless attempts, Deer had always been one step ahead, swift and graceful. But today, Wolf felt a new surge of determination.

"I must catch Deer today," Wolf muttered to himself, his ears pricked forward and his nose twitching as he sniffed the air for any sign of Deer.

Meanwhile, Deer was grazing in a meadow near a sparkling stream. The water flowed gently over smooth stones, and the sunlight danced on the surface. Deer nibbled on the sweet grass, always alert for any danger.

"I love this meadow," Deer thought, looking around. "But I must be careful. Wolf could be anywhere."

As Wolf crept closer to the meadow, he spotted Deer. His heart raced with excitement. "There you are, Deer," he whispered. "This time, you won't escape."

Wolf moved silently, his paws barely making a sound on the soft forest floor. He crouched low, ready to pounce. But just as he was about to leap, Deer's ears twitched. Deer sensed danger and sprang into action, bounding gracefully across the meadow.

"You won't catch me, Wolf!" Deer called over his shoulder, his voice light and teasing.

Wolf growled in frustration but did not give up. He chased Deer through the forest, his eyes fixed on his swift target. "I'll catch you, Deer! Just you wait!" Wolf shouted, pushing himself to run faster.

Deer zigzagged through the trees, his hooves barely touching the ground. He knew the forest well and used his knowledge to stay ahead. "You'll have to be quicker than that, Wolf!" Deer replied, smiling as he darted around a large oak tree.

Despite the chase, Wolf could not catch Deer. He finally stopped, panting and exhausted. "Why is it so hard to catch you?" Wolf asked, looking up at Deer, who had stopped a safe distance away.

Deer laughed softly. "Because I love my freedom, Wolf. And I know this forest like the back of my hoof."

Wolf sat down, catching his breath. "I understand, Deer. I dream of catching you, but you are always one step ahead."

Deer stepped closer, still cautious. "Maybe, Wolf, instead of always trying to catch me, we could find another way to live in this forest. There's enough for all of us."

Wolf thought about Deer's words. "Maybe you're right, Deer. But I can't change overnight. It's in my nature to hunt."

Deer nodded. "I know, Wolf. But perhaps we can learn to respect each other's strengths. We both want to live freely in this beautiful forest."

The forest grew quieter as the sun began to set, casting long shadows across the ground. Wolf and Deer stood there, each understanding the other a little better.

"Maybe one day, we can find a way to live peacefully," Deer said softly, before bounding away into the deep forest.

Wolf watched Deer disappear into the trees, feeling a mix of frustration and admiration. "Maybe one day," he echoed, turning to find his way back through the forest, the scent of pine and wildflowers still in the air.

3

The Eagle's Pursuit

High above the dense forest, Eagle soared gracefully through the clear blue sky. His sharp eyes scanned the ground below, always searching for his next meal. The sun's rays made his feathers gleam as he glided effortlessly on the wind.

"For years, I have watched you, Snake," Eagle thought as he circled high above. "One day, I will catch you."

Down on the forest floor, Snake moved quietly through the underbrush. His scales shimmered in the patches of sunlight that filtered through the trees. He was always on the lookout, his tongue flicking in and out, tasting the air.

"I must be careful," Snake said to himself. "Eagle is always watching."

The forest was alive with sounds. Birds chirped, and leaves rustled gently in the breeze. A gentle stream flowed nearby, its water sparkling in the sunlight. Snake paused for a moment to drink from the cool, clear stream, always keeping one eye on the sky.

Suddenly, a shadow passed overhead. Snake froze, his heart racing. "Eagle is near," he thought, slipping quickly into the cover of thick bushes.

From above, Eagle spotted the movement. "There you are, Snake," he said with a sharp cry, diving swiftly towards the ground. His powerful wings cut through the air as he aimed for Snake.

Snake moved quickly, weaving through the underbrush. His agility and cunning had kept him safe for years, but he knew he had to stay one step ahead. "Not today, Eagle," Snake whispered, slithering into a narrow crevice between rocks.

Eagle landed gracefully on a branch nearby, his keen eyes searching the ground. "You are clever, Snake," he said aloud. "But I am patient."

Snake peered out from his hiding spot, his body coiled tightly. "Why do you chase me, Eagle?" he asked, his voice a soft hiss.

Eagle tilted his head, his eyes never leaving Snake. "It is my nature to hunt, just as it is yours to hide. We each have our role in this forest."

Snake nodded slowly. "I understand, Eagle. But I wish for peace, just as you wish for a meal."

Eagle considered Snake's words. "Perhaps there is a way for us to co-exist," he said thoughtfully. "The forest is vast, and there is enough for all of us if we are wise."

Snake relaxed a little, sensing Eagle's sincerity. "Then let us agree to respect each other's space. I will stay out of the open, and you will hunt elsewhere."

Eagle nodded. "Very well, Snake. Let us try to live in harmony."

With that, Eagle spread his wings and took to the sky once more, soaring higher and higher until he was just a speck in the distance. Snake watched him go, feeling a sense of relief.

"Maybe there is hope for us all," Snake said quietly, emerging from his hiding place and continuing his journey through the forest.

The sun continued to shine brightly, casting a warm glow over the forest. The sounds of nature filled the air, and a sense of peace settled over the land. Eagle and Snake had reached an understanding, showing that even the most unlikely of creatures could find a way to coexist.

4

A Chance Meeting

One fateful day, the sun shone brightly over the forest, casting a golden glow on everything it touched. Birds chirped happily, and a gentle breeze rustled the leaves. Near a sparkling river, Deer was grazing on the lush green grass, enjoying the peaceful morning.

"This grass is so sweet and fresh," Deer thought, his ears twitching as he listened to the sounds of the forest.

Suddenly, there was a rustling in the grass nearby. Deer lifted his head, his heart pounding with surprise. Out from the tall grass slithered Snake, his scales glistening in the sunlight. Both Deer and Snake froze, startled by each other's presence.

"Hello, Deer," Snake hissed softly, trying to calm himself. "I didn't mean to startle you."

Deer took a cautious step back but nodded. "Hello, Snake. You surprised me. I was just enjoying this beautiful day."

Snake coiled himself comfortably on a rock by the river, keeping his distance. "I came to bask in the sun. It's nice and warm today," he said, flicking his tongue to taste the air.

Deer relaxed a little, sensing no danger. "It's a lovely day," he agreed. "But I always have to be careful. Wolf has been trying to catch me for a long time."

Snake nodded. "I know how you feel. Eagle has been hunting me for years. It's exhausting trying to stay hidden all the time."

Deer looked at Snake with empathy. "It sounds like we both have a lot to worry about."

Snake sighed. "Yes, but maybe we can help each other. If we stick together, we might be able to protect each other from Wolf and Eagle."

Deer thought for a moment and then nodded eagerly. "That sounds like a good idea, Snake. We can watch out for each other."

Snake smiled, and a sense of relief washed over him. "Let's make a pact, then. I'll help you if Wolf is near, and you can warn me if Eagle is around."

Deer extended his hoof, and Snake gently touched it with his tail. "It's a deal," Deer said with a smile.

From that day on, Deer and Snake became unlikely friends. They roamed the forest together, always keeping an eye out for danger. Deer would warn Snake if he saw Eagle soaring overhead, and Snake would alert Deer if he sensed Wolf nearby.

Their friendship grew stronger with each passing day. Every morning, Deer and Snake would meet by the river, where the water sparkled in the sunlight and the air was filled with the sweet scent of flowers. They would share stories of their adventures and their dreams, finding comfort in each other's company.

"I never thought I could feel so safe," Deer said one morning as he nibbled on the fresh grass. "Knowing you are watching out for me gives me so much peace."

Snake smiled, his scales shimmering in the sunlight. "And I feel the same, Deer. With you by my side, I don't have to worry about Eagle as much."

They found joy in the simple things, like basking in the warm sun. Deer would lie on the soft grass, soaking up the warmth, while Snake coiled up nearby, enjoying the gentle rays. The forest seemed more beautiful and alive when they were together, with birds singing cheerful songs and butterflies fluttering around.

In the evenings, as the sun began to set, they would walk together through the forest, exploring new paths and discovering hidden spots. They laughed and played, feeling free and happy. Their laughter echoed through the trees, creating a melody of friendship that even the wind seemed to carry.

5

The Pact of Protection

The forest was filled with the sounds of chirping birds and the rustling of leaves in the gentle breeze. Deer and Snake sat by the sparkling river, their reflections dancing on the water's surface. The air was warm, and the scent of flowers filled the air.

"Snake, we need to protect each other," Deer said, his eyes serious. "I can run fast and see danger from far away. I can warn you if Wolf is near."

Snake nodded, his tongue flicking out. "And I have my cunning and venom. I can help you if you are ever in trouble. Together, we can keep each other safe."

Deer extended his hoof, and Snake wrapped his tail around it. "It's a promise," Deer said.

"Yes, a promise," Snake agreed.

From that day on, Deer and Snake were always on the lookout for danger. One sunny afternoon, as they were walking through the forest, Deer suddenly stopped. His ears twitched, and he looked around nervously.

"What's wrong, Deer?" Snake asked, sensing the tension.

"I think I heard something," Deer whispered. "It might be Wolf. We need to hide."

Snake quickly found a thick bush, and they both slipped under its cover. They waited, holding their breath, as the forest grew silent.

After a few moments, the sound of heavy footsteps reached their ears. Wolf appeared, sniffing the air and looking around.

"I can smell Deer," Wolf growled softly to himself. "He must be close."

Deer trembled, but Snake stayed calm. "Stay still, Deer. Wolf won't find us here," Snake whispered.

Wolf sniffed around for a while longer, but unable to find Deer, he eventually gave up and walked away. Deer and Snake waited until they were sure Wolf was gone before emerging from their hiding spot.

"Thank you, Snake," Deer said, his voice filled with gratitude. "I was so scared."

"You did well, Deer," Snake replied. "We stayed safe because we worked together."

Another time, as they were near the river, Snake sensed danger. "Deer, I smell Eagle. We need to be careful."

Deer looked up and saw the shadow of Eagle circling overhead. "Let's move under the trees," Deer suggested.

They quickly moved to the cover of the trees, where the thick branches hid them from Eagle's sight. They watched as Eagle soared by, unaware of their presence.

"That was close," Deer said with a sigh of relief.

"Yes, but we managed to stay safe," Snake replied. "Remember, we need to trust each other."

Their bond grew stronger with each passing day, built on trust and mutual survival. They found joy in their friendship and the safety it brought. Other animals in the forest noticed their bond and began to learn from them.

Fox, who had seen them hide from Wolf, approached one day. "How do you do it?" he asked. "How do you stay so safe?"

"We trust each other," Deer explained. "We use our strengths to protect one another."

Fox nodded, impressed. "Maybe I can do the same with my friends."

The forest became a safer place, with animals helping and protecting each other. Deer and Snake's story spread, and they became symbols of trust and cooperation.

One evening, as the sun set and the forest was bathed in a warm golden light, Deer and Snake sat by the river, watching the sky turn shades of pink and orange.

"We've come a long way," Deer said, smiling at his friend.

"Yes, we have," Snake agreed. "And together, we can face anything."

They stayed by the river, enjoying the peace and knowing that, no matter what, they had each other's backs.

6

Wolf's Dilemma

The forest was a symphony of life. The leaves whispered secrets to the wind, the river murmured a soothing lullaby, and the birds sang cheerful songs from their perches high in the trees. Yet, amidst this harmony, Wolf was frustrated. He prowled through the underbrush, his senses on high alert.

"Where could Deer be hiding?" Wolf muttered, his sharp eyes scanning the dense foliage. "He used to be so easy to find."

Wolf's days were spent tracking Deer, but something had changed. No matter how hard he tried, Deer seemed to vanish just as he got close. It was as if Deer had become a ghost, always one step ahead.

Meanwhile, high above the forest canopy, Eagle soared on the thermals, his keen eyes sweeping the ground below. The sunlight gleamed off his feathers as he glided effortlessly through the air. But even with his superior vision, he was struggling.

"Where is Snake hiding?" Eagle wondered, his voice carried away by the wind. "He used to be so easy to spot."

Eagle had spent days circling the forest, but Snake remained elusive, slipping through the shadows and blending seamlessly with his surroundings. Eagle's patience was wearing thin.

One afternoon, as the sun began its descent, casting long shadows across the forest floor, Wolf and Eagle met at the edge of a clearing. The golden light bathed everything in a warm glow, but their moods were anything but sunny.

"Have you noticed something strange, Eagle?" Wolf asked, sitting on a large rock and scratching behind his ear with his paw. "Deer has become so hard to catch."

Eagle landed gracefully on a sturdy branch above Wolf, his wings folding neatly against his body. "Yes, Wolf. Snake has also become much harder to find. It's like they know we're coming."

Wolf nodded, his brow furrowing. "Something has changed in the forest. But what?"

Eagle tilted his head, thinking deeply. "Maybe they're working together. I've seen Deer and Snake together more often lately."

Wolf's eyes widened in surprise. "Working together? But they're so different!"

Eagle nodded. "Yes, but maybe that's why it's working. They use each other's strengths to stay safe."

Wolf growled softly, deep in thought. "We need to find a way to outsmart them. But how?"

As they pondered, the forest around them grew darker. Shadows lengthened, and a sense of suspense filled the air. The wind whispered through the trees, carrying with it the secrets of the forest. The sounds of the forest seemed to grow quieter as if even the animals were waiting to see what would happen next.

Meanwhile, hidden in a dense thicket not far from where Wolf and Eagle talked, Deer and Snake listened carefully. They had grown accustomed to moving silently and blending into their surroundings. Every rustle and whisper of the forest was a warning to them.

"They're talking about us," Deer whispered, his ears twitching nervously. The soft light filtered through the leaves, creating a dappled pattern on his fur.

Snake nodded, his scales shimmering in the fading light. "Yes, but as long as we stay together and watch out for each other, we'll be safe."

Deer smiled, feeling a bit more at ease. "I'm glad we're friends, Snake. Together, we can face anything."

Snake coiled protectively around Deer, his eyes gleaming with determination. "And I feel the same, Deer. We'll stay one step ahead of them."

As night fell, the forest was bathed in a silvery glow from the rising moon. Wolf and Eagle decided to call off their search for the day, each resolving to come up with a new plan.

"We'll catch them eventually," Wolf said to himself, his voice a low growl as he trotted back to his den. The path was familiar, but tonight it seemed filled with unseen obstacles and unknown challenges.

"And we'll find a way," Eagle agreed, his voice a whisper in the wind as he soared back to his nest high in the treetops. The moonlight reflected off his feathers, making him appear almost ghostly against the night sky.

The forest was left in peace, the stars twinkling above and the moon casting a gentle glow over the land. Deer and Snake remained vigilant, their bond stronger than ever. They found a secluded spot near the river, where the water's gentle flow provided a soothing backdrop to their whispered conversations.

"We need to keep practicing our hiding," Deer said, his voice barely audible over the river's murmur. "Wolf and Eagle are getting smarter."

Snake nodded. "Yes, we must stay alert and use the forest to our advantage. Every tree, every shadow is our ally."

The forest creatures watched and learned from Deer and Snake, understanding that friendship and cooperation were powerful tools. Fox, who had once been skeptical of alliances, now sought out others to form his own partnerships.

"I saw how Deer and Snake work together," Fox said one evening to Rabbit. "Maybe we can do the same."

Rabbit, who had always been quick and clever, nodded. "Yes, Fox. We can watch out for each other."

Wolf and Eagle, though formidable, were no match for the trust and unity shared by Deer and Snake. Their partnership became a legend among the forest creatures, a story of how two unlikely friends changed the dynamics of their world.

As the nights grew longer and the days cooler, the forest began to prepare for winter. The animals worked together, gathering food and finding shelter, inspired by the example set by Deer and Snake.

One crisp morning, as frost glittered on the grass and the air was filled with the promise of snow, Wolf and Eagle met once again at the clearing's edge.

"I haven't caught Deer," Wolf admitted, his breath visible in the cold air.

"And I haven't found Snake," Eagle replied, his voice tinged with frustration.

Wolf sighed, his eyes scanning the horizon. "Maybe we need to change our ways."

Eagle looked thoughtful. "Perhaps. The forest is changing, and so must we."

As they parted ways, each lost in their thoughts, the forest continued to thrive under the moonlight and the stars. Deer and Snake watched from their hidden spot, knowing that as long as they had each other, they could face any challenge.

7

〰

A Test of Friendship

The sun was high in the sky, casting a warm glow over the dense forest. The river flowed gently, its water sparkling under the sunlight. Birds chirped cheerfully, and the scent of blooming flowers filled the air. Deer was grazing near the riverbank, enjoying the peace and quiet.

"This is such a beautiful day," Deer thought, munching on the sweet grass. "I hope Snake is having a good day too."

Unbeknownst to Deer, Wolf had been watching him from the

shadows. Wolf's eyes gleamed with hunger and determination. He had been tracking Deer for days, waiting for the perfect moment to strike. Today, he felt, was that day.

Wolf crept closer, his body low to the ground, moving silently through the underbrush. His heart pounded with anticipation. He could almost taste his victory.

"Today, you won't escape, Deer," Wolf whispered to himself, his eyes locked on his prey.

Deer continued to graze, unaware of the danger lurking nearby. The gentle rustling of the leaves and the soft murmur of the river masked Wolf's approach. But as Wolf prepared to pounce, a sudden movement caught his eye.

Snake had emerged from the grass, his tongue flicking in and out as he tasted the air. He sensed Wolf's presence and immediately understood the threat. Without hesitation, Snake slithered quickly towards Deer.

"Deer, watch out!" Snake hissed loudly, his body coiling defensively.

Deer lifted his head, startled by Snake's urgent warning. His eyes widened in fear as he saw Wolf ready to pounce. Panic surged through him, but before he could react, Snake placed himself between Deer and Wolf, hissing and baring his fangs.

"Stay back, Wolf!" Snake hissed, his eyes fierce. "You won't harm my friend!"

Wolf skidded to a halt, surprised by Snake's sudden appearance. His eyes narrowed, and he growled, feeling both anger and confusion. "Snake, why are you protecting Deer?" he demanded.

Snake's eyes never wavered. "Because Deer is my friend, and I will not let you harm him."

Wolf hesitated, taken aback by the sight of the united friends. He had expected an easy hunt, but now he faced two determined opponents. For a moment, Wolf and Snake stared at each other, the tension thick in the air.

Deer's heart pounded in his chest. He knew he had to act quickly. Taking advantage of Wolf's hesitation, Deer leaped away, bounding swiftly through the forest.

"Run, Deer!" Snake urged, keeping his eyes on Wolf. "I'll hold him off!"

Deer didn't need to be told twice. He sprinted through the trees, his hooves barely touching the ground. The forest blurred around him as he ran, his heart racing with both fear and gratitude.

Meanwhile, Snake stood his ground, his body coiled and ready to strike. Wolf took a cautious step forward, his eyes never leaving Snake.

"You're risking your life for Deer?" Wolf asked, his voice a low growl.

"Yes," Snake replied firmly. "Friendship is worth any risk."

Wolf's eyes flickered with uncertainty. He had never encountered such determination and loyalty before. Slowly, he backed away, realizing that today was not his day to win.

"Very well, Snake," Wolf said, his voice begrudgingly respectful. "But this isn't over."

Snake watched as Wolf retreated into the shadows, his body relaxing only when Wolf was out of sight. He turned to see Deer watching from a distance, his eyes filled with relief and gratitude.

"Thank you, Snake," Deer said, his voice trembling with emotion. "You saved my life."

Snake slithered over to Deer, his eyes softening. "That's what friends do, Deer. We protect each other."

Deer nodded, his heart swelling with gratitude. "I will never forget this, Snake. You are a true friend."

Together, Deer and Snake made their way back to their favorite spot by the river. The sun was beginning to set, casting a golden glow over the water. They lay down side by side, their hearts beating in unison.

"Today was a test of our friendship," Deer said quietly, looking up at the sky.

"And we passed," Snake replied, his voice filled with pride. "Together, we are stronger than any danger."

As the stars began to twinkle above, the forest around them seemed to sigh with relief. The bond between Deer and Snake had grown even stronger, forged in the heat of danger and tested by the harsh realities of the forest.

The animals of the forest, having witnessed the bravery and loyalty of Deer and Snake, felt a renewed sense of hope and unity. They knew that with such strong examples of friendship, they too could find the strength to protect and support one another.

From that day on, Deer and Snake's friendship became a legend in the forest, a tale of courage, loyalty, and the power of true friendship. And as they lay by the river, basking in the peaceful night, they knew that no matter what challenges lay ahead, they would always have each other.

as they lay by the river, basking in the peaceful night, they knew that no matter what challenges lay ahead, they would always have each other.

8

❧

Eagle's Lesson

High above the forest, Eagle soared gracefully on the wind currents. His sharp eyes scanned the ground below, always on the lookout for his next meal. The sun was beginning to set, casting a warm golden glow over the treetops. As he circled above, Eagle noticed a commotion near the river.

"What's happening down there?" Eagle wondered, adjusting his flight path to get a better view.

Below, the unfolding drama between Wolf, Deer, and Snake caught his attention. He watched as Snake bravely defended Deer from Wolf, standing his ground with fierce determination. Eagle admired Snake's courage and the loyalty between the two friends.

"Snake has allies now," Eagle thought. "That makes him a much more challenging prey."

Eagle perched on a high branch, observing the scene below. The forest was quiet, the tension thick in the air. Wolf eventually backed away, realizing he couldn't win against the united front of Deer and Snake.

"Friendship gives them strength," Eagle mused, watching as Deer and Snake moved back to the riverbank, their bond even stronger after the encounter.

Eagle admired their friendship and the way they protected each other. He thought about his own life, always hunting and living alone. Seeing Deer and Snake made him realize the power of unity and support.

"Perhaps there's more to life than just hunting," Eagle said to himself. "Maybe I can find other prey and give Snake a chance to live peacefully."

Eagle spread his wings and took to the sky again, the wind ruffling his feathers. He soared high above the forest, contemplating his next move. The vast expanse of the forest stretched out below him, filled with potential prey. He knew he could find food elsewhere without disturbing the newfound peace of Snake and Deer.

As he flew, Eagle spotted a small group of mice scurrying through the underbrush. He decided to swoop down and catch one, his sharp talons closing around his target effortlessly. As he ascended with his meal, he glanced back at the river where Deer and Snake were resting.

"I'll let you have your peace, Snake," Eagle thought. "You deserve it."

Eagle returned to his nest, high in the tallest tree, and enjoyed his meal. The view from his perch was breathtaking, with the forest bathed in the soft light of the setting sun. He felt a sense of satisfaction, not just from his successful hunt, but from his decision to respect the bond between Snake and Deer.

The next day, as Eagle soared through the sky, he noticed other animals interacting below. Fox and Rabbit were working together to gather food, inspired by the example set by Deer and Snake. The forest seemed to be changing, becoming a place where cooperation and friendship thrived.

Eagle decided to visit Deer and Snake, curious to see how they were doing. He found them near the river, enjoying the calm and beauty of the morning.

"Good morning, Snake," Eagle called out as he landed gracefully on a nearby branch. "Deer."

Snake looked up, surprised but not alarmed. "Good morning, Eagle. What brings you here?"

Eagle nodded toward them. "I saw what happened with Wolf. You both showed great courage and loyalty. I wanted to tell you that I admire your friendship."

Deer stepped forward, his eyes bright with gratitude. "Thank you, Eagle. Your words mean a lot to us."

Eagle shifted his weight on the branch. "I've decided to respect your bond and find my prey elsewhere. You have my word that I won't disturb your peace."

Snake's eyes softened. "Thank you, Eagle. That means more than you know."

Eagle smiled, feeling a warmth in his chest that he hadn't felt in a long time. "We can all learn from each other. Even though we are different, we share this forest. Let's make it a place where everyone can live in harmony."

Deer and Snake nodded in agreement, their hearts swelling with hope. As Eagle took off into the sky once more, the forest felt like a brighter, more connected place.

From that day on, Eagle kept his promise. He found other prey and left Snake and Deer to enjoy their peace. The forest thrived with the spirit of cooperation, and the story of Eagle's lesson spread among the animals.

Fox, Rabbit, and many others began to form their own alliances, learning that together, they were stronger. The forest became a place of unity and mutual respect, all because of the brave actions of Snake, the loyalty of Deer, and the wisdom of Eagle.

As the days passed, the animals of the forest lived in harmony, each one playing their part in the delicate balance of life. Eagle's decision to let Snake live in peace was a turning point, teaching everyone that even the fiercest creatures could choose a path of understanding and respect.

And so, the legend of Deer, Snake, and Eagle was told and retold, becoming a cherished story that reminded all the forest inhabitants of the power of friendship and the importance of living together in harmony.

9

Harmony in the Forest

With Wolf and Eagle respecting the new alliance, the forest began to change. The days grew warmer, and the forest flourished under the golden sun. The once tense atmosphere was now filled with a sense of peace and unity. Deer and Snake's friendship had shown other animals that unity and cooperation could bring harmony.

One morning, as the sun's first rays filtered through the trees, Deer and Snake were resting by their favorite spot near the river. The air was fresh, and the gentle sound of the river flowing created a soothing melody.

"Look how peaceful the forest is now," Deer said, sipping the cool water. "It's hard to believe things were so different before."

Snake nodded, his eyes scanning the surroundings. "Our friendship made a difference, Deer. It showed everyone that we can live together peacefully."

As they enjoyed the serene morning, Fox approached cautiously, his ears twitching with curiosity. "Good morning, Deer and Snake," he greeted them. "I've noticed the change in the forest. Animals are working together more now."

Deer smiled warmly. "Good morning, Fox. Yes, the forest is different. Cooperation and friendship have made it better for all of us."

Fox sat down beside them, his tail curling around his feet. "I've seen Rabbit and Squirrel gathering food together. Even Owl and Mouse are sharing their wisdom and knowledge."

Snake flicked his tongue thoughtfully. "Unity brings strength, Fox. When we help each other, we all benefit."

As they talked, Wolf appeared at the edge of the clearing. He approached slowly, his head held low in a gesture of peace. "May I join you?" Wolf asked, his voice gentle.

Deer nodded. "Of course, Wolf. We're all friends here."

Wolf sat down, looking around at the peaceful scene. "I've learned a lot from watching you two. I realized that hunting isn't the only way to live. There's more to life than just surviving."

Snake slithered closer. "We're glad you see it that way, Wolf. Everyone has something to offer. Together, we make the forest a better place."

Eagle soared overhead, his sharp eyes taking in the scene below. He landed gracefully on a branch nearby and called down to them. "Good morning, friends. I've been watching from above, and I must say, the forest looks more beautiful now."

Deer looked up at Eagle, his eyes bright with happiness. "Good morning, Eagle. It's wonderful to see everyone getting along."

Eagle nodded. "Indeed. I've found other prey and left Snake and his friends in peace. Cooperation has its rewards."

As the sun climbed higher in the sky, more animals joined them by the river. Rabbit hopped over, carrying a bundle of fresh greens. Squirrel scampered down from a tree, his cheeks full of nuts. Even Bear lumbered out of the forest, his eyes twinkling with curiosity.

"We heard about the changes in the forest," Bear said, his deep voice rumbling. "We wanted to see for ourselves."

Deer welcomed them all with open arms. "Join us, everyone. We're celebrating a new era of harmony in the forest."

The animals gathered around, sharing stories and food. The air was filled with laughter and the sounds of happy chatter. They all realized that by helping each other, they had created a community where everyone thrived.

As the day turned into evening, the forest was bathed in a soft golden light. The stars began to twinkle in the sky, and a gentle breeze rustled the leaves. The animals settled down for the night, knowing they were safe and united.

"Today has been wonderful," Deer said, lying down beside Snake. "Our forest is a place of peace now."

Snake coiled up comfortably. "Yes, Deer. We've shown that even the most unlikely of friends can change the world."

From his perch, Eagle watched over the forest, his heart filled with pride. Wolf lay down nearby, feeling content for the first time in a long while. The sense of unity and friendship warmed their hearts as they drifted off to sleep.

The forest had entered a new era, one where cooperation and mutual respect reigned. The story of Deer and Snake's friendship spread far and wide, inspiring animals everywhere to seek harmony and peace.

As the forest thrived, the animals knew that they were part of something special. They had learned that together, they could overcome any challenge and create a world where everyone lived in harmony.

And so, the forest remained a place of beauty and peace, where the lessons of unity and friendship were passed down through generations. The tale of Deer, Snake, Wolf, and Eagle became a cherished legend, reminding all who heard it that true strength lies in cooperation and mutual respect.

10

The Legacy of Friendship

Years passed, and the bond between Deer and Snake remained as strong as ever. Their friendship had grown into a legendary tale that every young animal in the forest knew by heart. The story of Deer and Snake's loyalty and bravery was told and retold by the elders, becoming a timeless lesson about the power of friendship and cooperation.

One crisp autumn morning, as the leaves turned golden and red, Deer and Snake sat by their favorite spot near the river. The air was filled with the sweet scent of fallen leaves, and the gentle sound of the river flowing created a soothing backdrop to their conversation.

"Do you remember the day we first met by this river?" Deer asked, his eyes twinkling with fond memories.

"How could I forget?" Snake replied, flicking his tongue with a smile. "It was the day our lives changed forever."

Deer nodded, his heart swelling with gratitude. "We've come a long way since then. Look at how much the forest has changed."

Snake looked around, his eyes scanning the vibrant, bustling forest. Animals of all kinds were working together, helping each other and living in harmony. "Our friendship showed them the way. It's amazing to see everyone cooperating."

Just then, a group of young animals approached them. A curious fawn, a playful rabbit, a chatty squirrel, and a wide-eyed mouse gathered around Deer and Snake, their eyes filled with admiration.

"Will you tell us the story again?" the fawn asked eagerly. "We love hearing about how you became friends."

Deer chuckled softly. "Of course, we'd be happy to. It all started right here by this river, when Snake and I realized that we could protect each other from danger."

As Deer and Snake recounted their story, the young animals listened intently, their eyes wide with wonder. They heard about the challenges Deer and Snake had faced, the courage they had shown, and the strong bond that had formed between them.

"You see," Snake concluded, "true strength lies not in our differences, but in how we use those differences to help each other. Together, we are stronger than any danger."

The young animals nodded, their hearts filled with inspiration. They knew that they, too, could make a difference by working together and supporting one another.

Meanwhile, Wolf and Eagle watched from a distance, their hearts filled with pride and respect. They had also found new ways to thrive, understanding that there was more to life than just hunting.

Wolf approached the group, his demeanor calm and peaceful. "May I join you?" he asked, his voice gentle.

Deer smiled warmly. "Of course, Wolf. You are part of this story too."

Wolf sat down beside them, his eyes reflecting the golden light of the autumn sun. "I've learned so much from you both. I've found new ways to live in balance with others, and it's brought me a sense of peace I never knew before."

Eagle soared down from above, landing gracefully on a nearby branch. "And I, too, have found other prey and learned to respect the bonds of friendship. Life is better when we live in harmony."

The young animals looked up at Wolf and Eagle, their eyes filled with admiration and hope. They saw that even the fiercest creatures could change and find strength in unity.

As the sun began to set, casting a warm glow over the forest, the animals gathered together in a circle. They shared stories, laughed, and celebrated the harmony that had become the heart of their community.

Deer and Snake looked at each other, their hearts full of joy. "We've created something truly special here," Deer said softly.

"Yes, we have," Snake agreed. "And it will continue to grow, long after we're gone."

The forest thrived in this new era of cooperation and peace. Animals of all kinds worked together, supporting and protecting each other. The story of Deer and Snake's friendship became a cherished legend, a reminder that true strength comes from unity and mutual respect.

As the stars twinkled in the night sky, the forest was filled with the sounds of happy, contented animals. The lessons of friendship and cooperation had become the foundation of their lives, ensuring that the forest remained a place of beauty and peace.

And so, the legacy of Deer and Snake lived on, inspiring generations to come. Their story taught young animals that by working together and supporting one another, they could overcome any challenge and create a world where everyone thrived.

The forest, once a place of tension and danger, had transformed into a sanctuary of harmony. The tale of Deer, Snake, Wolf, and Eagle continued to be told, reminding all who heard it that true strength lies not in hunting alone, but in living in balance with others.

As the years passed, the bond between Deer and Snake remained unbreakable, a testament to the power of friendship. Their legacy lived on, a shining example of how cooperation and unity could change the world.

And so, the forest flourished, a place where every creature knew that they were stronger together. The story of Deer and Snake became a guiding light, showing that with friendship and cooperation, anything was possible.

www.ingramcontent.com/pod-product-compliance
Lightning Source LLC
Chambersburg PA
CBHW071255130726
47998CB00003B/1195